NOTE TO 1

Apologetics Press is a non-profit organization dedicated to the defense of New Testament Christianity. For over a quarter of a century, we have provided faith-building materials for adults. We also have produced numerous materials (like *Discovery* magazine, our *Explorer Series*, and various books) for young people in third grade through high school. We now are pleased to present a new series of books for even younger children.

The Apologetics Press Early Reader Series is a set of books aimed at children in kindergarten through second grade. Depending on the age of your children, this series is flexible enough to allow parents to read to their children, read along with their children, or they can listen while their children read aloud to them.

The books in this series are filled with beautiful full-color pictures and wonderful information about God, His creation, and His Word. These books are written on a level that early readers will enjoy, while drawing them closer to their Creator.

We hope you enjoy using the Apologetics Press Early Reader Series to encourage your children to read, while at the same time helping them learn about God and His creation.

God Made Insects

by Eric Lyons

Copyright © 2006
Apologetics Press

ISBN-10: 0-932859-86-0
ISBN-13: 978-0-932859-86-0

Library of Congress: 2005937137

Printed in China

God Made Insects

by
Eric Lyons

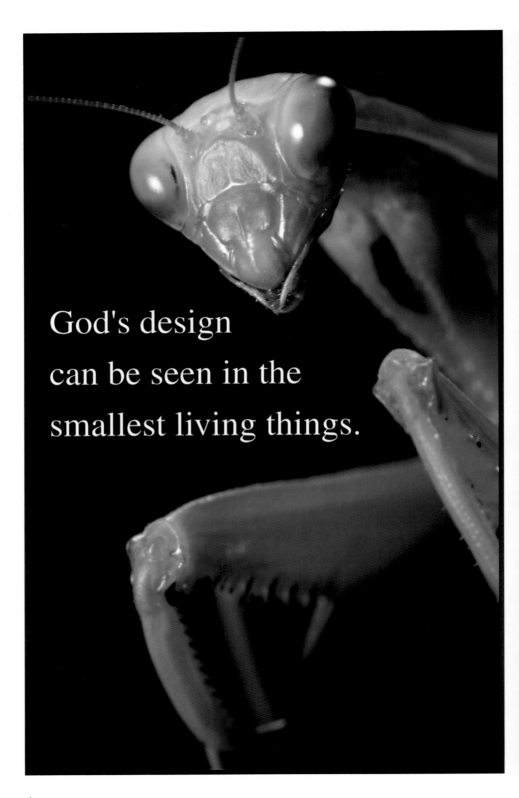

God's design
can be seen in the
smallest living things.

Take insects for an example.

The average insect
is less than one-half
of an inch long.

Ants are
a kind of insect
that are very
small.

But they are
also very strong.

God made ants so that they can pick up things 50 times their own weight.

That is like you being able to pick up a small car.

The biggest bug in the world
is the Goliath Beetle.

It can weigh as much as
a quarter-pound hamburger.

God made the bombardier beetle with a special defense system.

It can shoot a boiling hot spray out of its back end.

Photo by Thomas Eisner; used by permission

Termites eat wood.

They are good for the earth because they eat dead trees.

Sometimes they can also be pests, because they eat the wood in houses.

Dragonflies
can dash

forward
at
speeds
of
nearly
50 miles per hour.

God also gave them the ability
to fly straight up and down
like a helicopter.

This bug looks like it is praying. That is why it is called a praying mantis.

The praying
    mantis is really quick.
        It catches and eats flies.

God made some insects so that they blend in with nature.

Can you spot the caterpillar on this page?

The stick bug
is not only
hard to spot at
times, it is also
the longest
insect in the
world.

God designed spiders with
the amazing ability
to spin webs.

Pound for pound, the silk from certain kinds of spiders is five times stronger than steel.

The rhinoceros beetle has a horn-like structure on its head.

These horns are sometimes used when fighting other bugs.

Ladybugs are great
insects to have around.

They eat bugs that
attack vegetable crops.

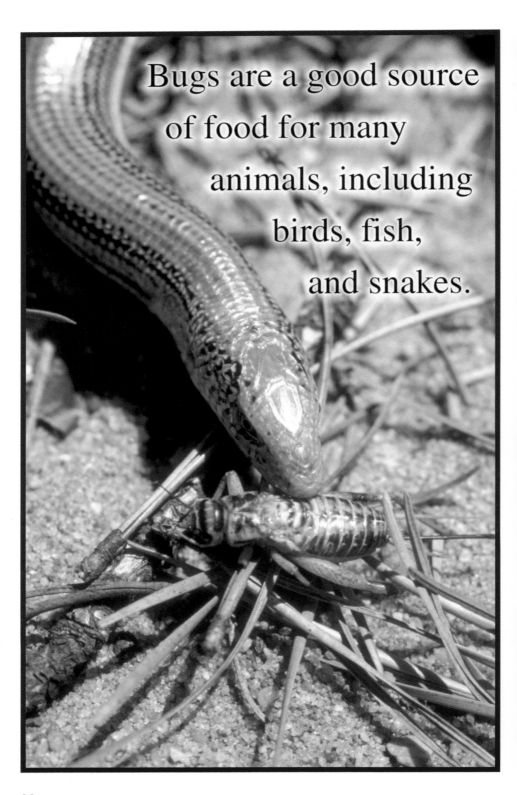

Bugs are a good source of food for many animals, including birds, fish, and snakes.

There are even people who eat bugs. Some people eat roasted termites like we eat popcorn.

One bug you do not want to eat is a stink bug.

As you can guess by its name, this bug puts out bad smells from its body.

The stinkbug's odor helps protect it from enemies.

Honeybees stay very busy making honey.

Some bees flap their wings 130 times in one second as they fly through the air.

Fireflies are
little beetles that
God made
which
carry
their own
flashlights.

These bugs make special chemicals that they put together with oxygen to create a bright light.

Butterflies are beautiful bugs that God created.

They come
in different
colors and
shapes.

Even though bugs are small in size, they are big on design.

Their design helps prove that God exists.